COUNTRY LIVING

SHOESTRING CHIC

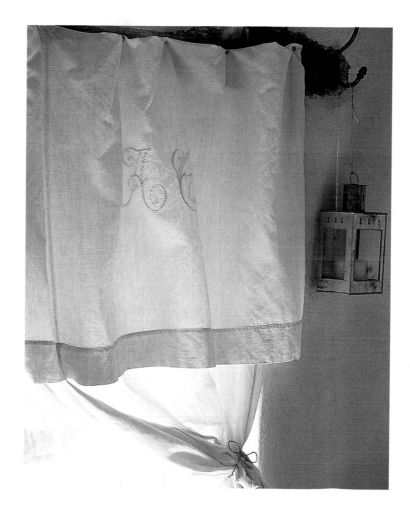

COUNTRY LIVING

SHOESTRING CHIC

EXTRAORDINARY STYLE FOR LESS

Gail Abbott

with special photography by Mark Scott

HEARST BOOKS
A Division of Sterling Publishing Co., Inc.
New York

Library of Congress Cataloging-in-Publication Data

Shoestring chic : extraordinary style for less.
    p. cm.
      At head of title: Country living.
      ISBN 1-58816-309-1
        1. Decoration and ornament, Rustic. 2. Interior decoration. I.
Country living (New York, N.Y.)

NK1986.R8S55 2004
747'1--dc22
                                          2003056915

10 9 8 7 6 5 4 3 2 1

Published by Hearst Books
A Division of Sterling Publishing Co., Inc.
387 Park Avenue South, New York, NY 10016

Country Living is a trademark owned by Hearst Magazines Property,
Inc., in USA, and Hearst Communications, Inc., in Canada.
Hearst Books is a trademark owned by Hearst Communications, Inc.

www.countryliving.com

Distributed in Canada by Sterling Publishing
c/o Canadian Manda Group, One Atlantic Avenue, Suite 105
Toronto, Ontario, Canada M6K 3E7
Distributed in Australia by Capricorn Link (Australia) Pty. Ltd.
P.O. Box 704, Windsor, NSW 2756 Australia

Printed in China

ISBN 1-58816-309-1
Designed by Christine Wood

CONTENTS

FOREWORD

If you're like me, coming up with decorating projects for your home is never a problem. However, finding the time and the resources to accomplish them can be. In *Shoestring Chic* we show you just how easy it is to enhance your home with decorative solutions that are simple to do and well within the reach of every budget. Throughout this book you'll discover inexpensive ways to add personal style to your home—room by room, whether your tastes are traditional, retro or modern. You'll see how a simple coat of paint can change the character of a room, create a backdrop for collectibles, or revive a neglected thrift-store find. If your handy, vintage and remnant fabrics picked up at sale prices can be fashioned into decorative cushions, seat covers and simple curtains for bedroom, bath or kitchen. Since shoestring decorating is all about mixing and matching and using objects in unusual ways, don't overlook the beauty of found items—like sea glass, stones, or buttons—to create a beautiful collection or mismatched china to set an unusual table. By being flexible and creative in your thinking, you'll be able to take advantage of bargains wherever they can be found. *Shoestring Chic* is nothing more than coming up with low-cost solutions that make a house easy to live in and that look beautiful, too. I hope this book inspires you to realize your dreams and how affordable they can be.

—NANCY MERNIT SORIANO, Editor-in-Chief *Country Living*

HALLS AND LIVING ROOMS

Just a few signature items can create the homespun feel of the country. All you need is an eye for detail and a little loving care.

A line-up of Shaker-style pegs displaying a collection of summer hats and a mix of knitted, floral, and striped cushions scattered along a painted wooden bench all say "welcome home" as soon you step through the door. Finishing touches to cushions, such as hand-tied bows (see left), add accent and texture.

Whether you live in a family house in the country or a tiny, modern apartment in the city, the entrance to your home can be made more welcoming and inviting. In this light and airy hall, the restrained use of pale colors and creative combinations of objects and furniture set a country theme and lighten the feel of the whole home.

For instant color any time of year, simply arrange a platter of fruits or vegetables to decorate those little neglected spaces in the home. To cheer up an ignored corner of a hall in winter, display a row of oranges on a windowsill; in the fall, a plate of pumpkins creates a feast of color on a hall table. These flourishes are a natural reminder of the changing of the seasons, and keep every corner of the house visually interesting, no matter how small.

It's always the unexpected details that make the most impact.

Collections of objects, either found on the beach or picked up over

the years while hunting through flea markets, can make stunning

displays to be enjoyed every time you meander through the rooms.

On the facing page, a row of old wooden shoe lasts look charming

placed on a shelf high above a staircase, while whimsical displays of

beach pebbles and glass are informal reminders of summer vacations.

INTRODUCING COLOR

If there's one color that says "shoestring chic," it's white. White paint is inexpensive, guarantees a room that's filled with light, and provides a pure, uncluttered backdrop against which you can blend old and new furniture. For rustic simplicity, expose the texture of the floor by adding white to the wood. You can treat pale, sanded floorboards with a wash of white water-based paint, then seal them with two or three coats of acrylic varnish. It's a subtle effect, in which every ounce of available light gets reflected around the whole room.

Even the coolest all-white interior can benefit from a splash or two of color to bring it to life and accentuate the details. One of the simplest ways to incorporate color is to set a vase of vibrant flowers on the table. You can pick them from the garden or buy them from the market, and arrange them in bunches of the same shade. Bright cushions and throw rugs are another instant way to bring a room to life, and can be easily changed at a later date. For truly individual cushion covers, sew together your fabric remnants, or go hunting for scraps at sales. You could also search thrift shops for a single, beautifully colored velvet curtain and cut it up to make a set of matching covers. Vintage buttons stitched to the corners add a bohemian touch. A store-bought blanket makes a cozy throw that can be snuggled up in on cool evenings.

LEFT: The owners of this old seaside cottage have exposed the original brickwork and floorboards, and given the white room brilliant touches of bright fuchsia, lime green, and blue using cushions, blankets, and a hand-painted niche.

If you have beautiful white objets d'art in your rooms, you can accentuate their simplicity by displaying them in color-washed niches or alcoves. Apply a wash of soft tones to the back wall of an alcove, choosing several colors that subtly blend together; you can keep built-in shelves pure white for emphasis. Or purchase a budget set of shelves for displaying beloved white china jugs and vases, and install the shelves against a niche wall painted in just one stunning color. These style ideas are also great for giving featureless rooms character and a focal point.

You can also bring in extra visual interest by using textural contrast. Even an unused wood stove, painted in a pale gray, looks wonderfully decorative against exposed brickwork in a modern apartment, and shows that vintage country style can look good in a modern setting.

RIGHT: The mellow tones of hand-made bricks contrast well with the gray wood stove and the white painted chest that acts as a coffee table. Bright pink camellias from the garden add a splash of color.

BELOW LEFT: These textured vases and bottles make a vibrant collection of shapes without adding color.

BELOW RIGHT: The soft, pastel colors suggest a seascape and make a colorful backdrop for the vases and bottles.

CREATIVE DETAILS

Artists Peter Clark and Karen Nichol are masters of making the simple spaces in their early nineteenth-century house look cool and elegant. The rooms are painted white, while the high ceilings have been treated to a wash of soft color that extends to the top of the walls, giving the effect of a bank of clouds in the far distance. Bare floorboards, and windows devoid of busy fabrics, make the spacious rooms look even bigger. The pieces chosen by the couple, many of them found in thrift shops, have been cleverly restored or decorated so that they are displayed against the plain walls like wonderful objects in a gallery.

But this is a real family home, and the furniture here has to work for a living. This chest of drawers, found covered in oil and dirt at the back of a garage, has been cleaned, rubbed with white paint, and given a new set of handles. It holds everything from spools of thread to DVDs, and makes it possible for the living room to be kept clear of clutter. For a similar distressed look, you could take a modern pine piece and rub it down with sandpaper to remove any varnish from the surface. Use a white candle to rub wax around the edges of drawers and areas that would generally get the most wear and apply a thin coat of water-based white paint to the wood. Use fine sandpaper to rub over the paint after it's dry to reveal a glimpse of the wood beneath.

The ceiling is painted in a soft pastel shade; the color bleeds down the top of the wall.

A bare branch found on a winter walk makes a dramatic statement when placed against the white wall.

Drawer handles found in a Spanish market give this antique chest a more modern look.

A vintage Stars and Stripes, decorated with circles of beads, makes a dramatic and colorful seat cover.

HALLS AND LIVING ROOMS

Carefully chosen details add color and texture to a room without the need for expensive decoration. Rhinestone jewelry that is no longer worn has found a new life on living-room cushions. Sculptural, budding twigs make a stylish alternative to fresh flowers and create a modern contrast to the 1930's vases on either side of the mantel. So many shops pack their goods in the most exquisite shopping bags, that it seems a pity to throw them away. Here, they have been used as planters by placing potted flowers inside the bags.

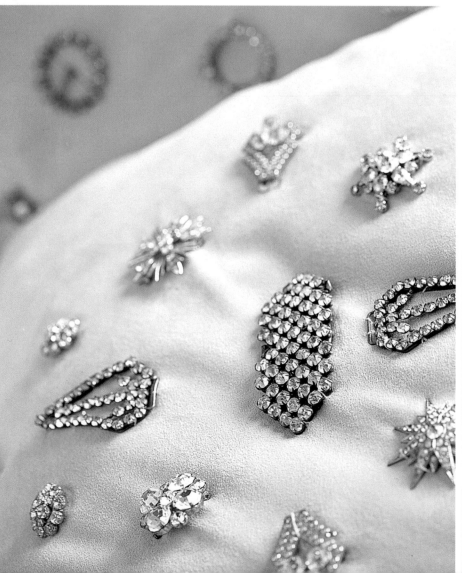

RIGHT: *A wall of unassuming shelving gives a dining room wall drama when it's stacked with a collection of plates. Displayed in color themes, the coordinating yellows, greens, and reds make ordinary plates look like something special.*

BELOW: *1950s fabric designers were often whimsical in their choice of motifs: from abstract shapes to garden tools and bottles of wine, the designs were fresh and fun, heralding a new design era for interiors. These fabrics are not easy to locate, but if you can uncover an original pair of curtains, for example, turn them into a set of cushions that are as delightful today as they were when they were printed.*

ABOVE: *China must be one of the easiest things to find when you're out hunting for treasures. Looking for pieces that match is one way to build up a set of retro china, but a mismatched, eclectic collection can be far more interesting. Odd plates, jugs, cups, and saucers may look uninspiring when they are relegated to the back of a dusty shelf, but can work well together in a display if you search out colors and patterns that catch your imagination.*

SHOESTRING ELEGANCE

Elegant living doesn't necessarily have to mean spending a fortune, and it's not difficult to give a small room the appearance of a traditional country drawing room. Soft whites combined with tarnished brass, faded florals, and stripes look comfortable and elegant, but can be achieved on a tight budget. Seek out bargains, and let "simplicity" and "faded" be your guiding principles.

Too many patterns and colors can look busy and overwhelm a small room. For example, you might choose white or neutrals for walls and your main furnishings, such as the sofa and chairs. Two contrasting shades often make the best accent colors—using just one color can make a room look two-dimensional; try a combination of soft reds and blues, if you prefer, or perhaps a mix of lavender and green.

A washed-out, faded look is the second key to country style. You could begin with fabric of a combination of stripes and faded florals, and make plenty of cushions to pile onto the sofa. Setting a gilded mirror on the mantelpiece will add a touch of glamour, and if it's a bit battered, so much the better. If you can't find an old one, make one from a molded picture frame. Replace the glass with a mirror and paint the frame gold, giving it a distressed look by rubbing off some of the paint before it's completely dry. Tarnished candlesticks and a simple flower arrangement complete the look.

ABOVE: *The original fireplace in this tiny living room was given a new wooden mantel and painted in glossy white eggshell. An old brass chandelier was rewired and gives a look of subdued grandeur to the room.*

OPPOSITE: *This worn sofa has been covered with a pale bedspread—it's one of the quickest solutions around when it comes to updating a room. The alcoves have been left empty to give the illusion of space. The matchboarding lining the walls of the alcoves adds texture to the room.*

LEFT: *A slatted cover made from fiberboard and battens was painted to match the walls and makes a simple solution to a common decorating problem—what to do about less-than-beautiful radiators. The cover allows warm air to circulate and makes a useful display shelf.*

OPPOSITE: *Mix old fabrics with new for cushions that will make your sofa a real comfort zone. Vintage linen has been hand-printed with soft, free-form roses and mixes beautifully with a modern version of traditional French mattress ticking. The inset monogram was taken from the top of a hand-embroidered sheet that was turned into a pair of curtains.*

When you're decorating on a shoestring, the more work you can do yourself, the better. Learning basic carpentry skills will save you money if you use your know-how to put up shelves or make a simple radiator cover. Also, you can design your projects just the way you want them, according to your taste. Making your own cushion covers is a good way to learn basic sewing techniques, and you can spoil yourself by buying small amounts of gorgeous fabric that might be too expensive to use on the windows.

Full of treasured memories, favorite possessions sit side by side on a drop-leaf table. Years of polishing have given it a deep, aged patina. The table acts as an informal bookshelf, too, where dog-eared paperbacks are stacked for easy reading. But the "antique" lamp has a new turned wood base—before being sanded and waxed, its old-world look was achieved with crackle glaze and water-based emulsion paint.

Inexpensive mementos and heirlooms can be appreciated every day if they are kept on display. On the mantel, an old china teacup cradles special items.

BREAKING THE BOUNDARIES

A hand-painted Roman blind at the window lets in plenty of light while providing privacy in this living room.

Hand-painted vertical wave patterns going across the walls give the room a gentle, misty ambience.

The sofa is wrapped in layers of textiles: a woven fabric from Africa is thrown over a linen sheet and softened with a mohair blanket and a couple of faux leather cushions.

Holding center stage in this room is this 1950's wicker coffee table, which adds a lively texture.

Don't let conventional ideas of design hold you back. When decorator Annabel Grey was asked to design a living room in this Arts and Crafts house, built in 1901, she wanted to create a room that was totally individual rather than re-create its original period look. A large and cold-looking space, the challenge was to link different areas of the room. Annabel created a comfortable living area, with a roaring wood fire, that opens onto a brick loggia looking out onto the garden. Earthy colors and ethnic textiles were juxtaposed layer upon layer to provide a richly patterned interior against subtle, wave-painted walls that seem to melt the edges of the space.

Breaking the bounds of mainstream design means that you can follow your heart when it comes to buying furniture and objects for your rooms. Consider pieces that other people may pass by—they may look unremarkable at first glance, but by linking their colors and textures you can allow them to co-exist comfortably side by side.

LEFT: Make a focal point of a simple object. Fake leather, fur, and animal fabrics are all incorporated into this patchwork cushion and look stunning on the striped velvet armchair.

ABOVE: *Wave-patterned walls were painted in vertical swaths of off-white and cream that subtly change all around the room.*

LEFT: *Paint or print on inexpensive fabrics for a unique look. Here, cotton duck fabric is hand-painted with sea birds in gray and brown.*

RIGHT: *The winged arms of these 1950's wicker chairs reflect the soaring shapes on the curtains.*

A twig wreath from the local florist was the only item purchased for this display, and can be used year after year.

A scattering of pine cones picked up on a winter walk keeps your interior in touch with nature and adds an air of informality.

A pile of logs brings the woods indoors into your country sanctuary, and feeds the fire all night.

COUNTRY CHRISTMAS

Christmas is also a time to sit back and relax with a good book. Keep books close at hand on a coffee table that doubles as a bookshelf.

Worlds away from mass-produced festivities, a country Christmas can be celebrated at home with natural, handmade objects that the family can gather from the garden and put up together. No matter how young, children can help collect materials for the holiday. Ivy and eucalyptus from the garden, apples from the orchard, and pine cones from the forest are simply laid along the mantelpiece around a large twig wreath. Light a pair of chunky candles and a roaring fire, and you will have the perfect backdrop for a memorable family gathering.

If you are handy with a sewing machine, you can make all your own gifts at a fraction of the price that they would cost in a store, and you can avoid the seasonal crowds at the same time. Thrift shop bargains include old woolen blankets whose subtle woven stripes make interesting borders that can be cut and patched together. Rummage through your rag bag to find small remnants of patchwork fabrics, buttons, and ribbons that you may have left over from larger projects.

Cushions, soft toys, and even Christmas stockings are a delight to make. Others will appreciate your special gifts for their uniqueness and the time you spent creating them.

ABOVE LEFT: Wrap presents in brown paper and tie them with ribbons for a thrifty, but stylish, wrapping solution.

ABOVE RIGHT: Made from scraps, this Christmas angel is beautifully simple with her wool hair and striped gown.

RIGHT: With its stripes pointing in different directions, a worn-out blanket gets a new lease on life as a recycled cushion cover.

DINING ROOMS

Clever bargain items and
an imaginative touch make
a beautiful dining room
that's perfect for a family
supper or a special meal
with friends.

SPECIAL OCCASIONS

It's not every day that you invite friends and family over for a festive meal, but when you do, a pretty table setting shows just how much you appreciate their company. Choose glasses that sparkle, well-polished cutlery, and simple flowers and candles to transform a workaday room into a delectable place to dine.

It's best to plan ahead when you are expecting guests, so try to prepare the dining room well in advance. You can treat yourself to a few hours' downtime, creatively mixing and matching old plates, cutlery, and glasses for an original, sumptuous look. If you look carefully, you can find beautiful old tableware that might be a little past its best, but will grace any special occasion—without the need to supplement it with expensive china.

Use clever cheats when it comes to expanding your dining space—tricks that give an impression of grandeur without breaking the bank. Substitute your usual dining table with a longer trestle, disguised under a large white sheet rather than a tablecloth. Starched and pressed, it will look impressive and special.

LEFT: *Only a few pieces of the cutlery, glassware, and china in this pretty spring tablesetting actually come from matching sets. The secret of its unified design lies in the abundance of fresh flowers, the crisp white sheet used as a tablecloth, and the extra touches, such as coordinated napkins and elegant candles.*

LEFT: *If a profusion of fresh flowers is beyond your budget, a single bright bloom in a pretty colored drinking glass is enough to make any meal table look dazzling.*

When it comes to setting a special-occasion table, you can't beat a beautiful arrangement of flowers. But they don't have to cost a lot to make a real impact. You can use a pressed-glass jug as a vase and tightly pack it with simple blooms like tulips, hyacinths, and gerbera daises, and then add a few sprigs of rosemary for texture. You can rent wine glasses by the day if you don't have enough for a large group of guests, or use a cheerfully mismatched set, sparklingly clean and polished, that look wonderful by candlelight. Make a point of using china and cutlery that has been picked up for a song: bone-handled knives, silver-plated forks and spoons, and a variety of dinner plates. You can add a finishing touch to plain napkins by tying them with a length of ribbon threaded with a tiny button.

CONTEMPORARY COUNTRY

Country living doesn't have to mean scrubbed tabletops, gingham, and baskets. There are many other ways of giving a room a country feel while on a budget.

This traditional room has white walls and stripped floorboards, curtainless windows, and clean lines that let light flood in throughout the day. But the secret of its upbeat, contemporary look is a well-considered color palette and an absence of distracting patterns. Cool, ice-blue paint on the woodwork and a bowl of oranges on the table act as complementary colors, enhancing one another's vibrancy in close proximity. The same goes for the vase of red tulips and the giant green-glass sculptures, made by the artist-owner, that fill the corner. Because red and green are opposite one another on the color wheel, they are guaranteed to stand out.

Painting a room all white is a great way to enhance light and make the most of a dining room with a high ceiling, especially if it still has its original fireplace. But without adding a little color, white can look too stark. If you have lovely old detailing on your windows, you could paint the frames in a pale shade to accentuate their charm. Or add furniture like a simple office table picked up in a secondhand store or a set of contemporary leather chairs for depth and texture— the combination of old and new is stunning but simple.

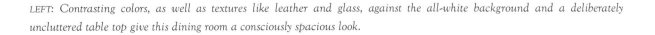

LEFT: Contrasting colors, as well as textures like leather and glass, against the all-white background and a deliberately uncluttered table top give this dining room a consciously spacious look.

The huge old mirror above the sideboard reflects all the light from the window. Its lavender-painted frame creates a warm contrast with the white walls.

Bottles and vases make a stunning display in front of the mirror. Each contains just one perfect bloom whose effect is doubled when reflected in the glass.

White china bowls, both old and new, filled with a medley of fruit add more vibrant color to the marble countertop.

EASTER BREAKFAST

When Easter Sunday comes around, it's time to celebrate a holy day in the Christian calendar and to honor the budding of a new season. The welcome arrival of spring flowers, the leaving behind of the long, cold winter, and a return to longer days are all marked with a simple but special breakfast with the family before a chocolate Easter egg hunt out in the garden. It's also a perfect opportunity for children to hand-paint their own eggs as a surprise for everyone when they come to the table in the morning. You can rise to the occasion with a blend of fun colors and textiles—such as a checkered tablecloth, spotted china, and a nest of tiny, sugar-coated eggs. If you are feeling creative, plant some spring flowers in terracotta pots that you've painted with water-based paint left over from decorating the house. Pots in pale, spun-sugar colors look wonderful planted with tiny daffodils, and make a lively splash of color on a window ledge.

LEFT: *Just for fun, decorate a plain, nylon-mesh food cover with a trim of feathers, and keep flies away from your favorite Danish pastry.*

RIGHT: *This simple seaside dining room opens off the kitchen and is just the place for a celebratory breakfast. Vivid orange gerbera daises and colorful spotted china make the table bright and fresh for a sunny Easter morning. The blue-and-green painted chairs and striped cushions pick up the colors in the checked tablecloth.*

Easter is just the time to get creative with paints and simple crafts, even if you never wield a brush at any other time of year. Find out how relaxing and therapeutic it can be to hold a perfectly oval egg in your hands and feel its shape, and to choose colors with all the careful concentration of a child. If you don't take it too seriously, you'll be surprised at how you can rediscover the lost pleasure of looking at colors and patterns. If decorated eggs are too time-consuming, build a tiny nest of chocolate eggs or simply paint jelly jars to use as vases.

FAR LEFT: *For a cute Easter centerpiece, build a nest with a tiny twig wreath bought at the local florist. Place it on a plate and fill it with chocolate eggs. Trim it with a real feather for a touch of authenticity.*

LEFT: *First, hard-boil six eggs and then leave them to cool. Paint each egg with water-based acrylic paints. Rest each one in an egg cup while you paint one side with spots of various colors and then fill in the centers with another shade. Turn the egg over when it's dry and paint the other end.*

RIGHT: *Wash terracotta plant pots and leave them to dry. Paint them inside and out with an undercoat of white water-based emulsion paint. Allow to dry. Paint the insides with pastel shades and the outsides with contrasting colors. Plant ready-grown spring flowers by repotting from plastic pots.*

FRENCH COUNTRY

Tucked away in small country towns, junkyards and thrift shops often contain pieces that no one else wants. To get the most out of your newfound treasures, be prepared to give them a new purpose. The owner of this traditional farmhouse in the Aveyron district of southern France has found clever ways to reuse things most people wouldn't give a second glance to. Within a strictly limited budget, she has given her rustic house charm and style by making frequent visits to the local flea markets, searching for the most interesting pieces. To get the same look, be prepared to spend ample time, and don't be disheartened if you come away empty-handed from your first foray into a junkyard. Good bargain-hunting takes dedication and an eagle eye, so keep it up and revisit sources time and again: You'll soon acquire some special finds.

A battered trestle table once used in the garden, country chairs with rush seating that have seen better days, or an enamel jug pressed into service as a flower vase all might look out of place in a smart city apartment, but in a rustic vacation house, seem very much at home.

With a painted floor scattered with Kelim rugs and wide-open French doors letting in the warm outdoor air, this converted farmhouse dining room has retained all the charm that the owners loved when they first saw it.

KITCHENS

For a retro, farmhouse, or
Shaker look, a little paint
and junkyard finds are all
you need to create a country
kitchen that's uniquely you.

RETRO STYLE

When you move into a new house or apartment, it's tempting to want to rip out the old kitchen and install a new one. But before you do, take a long look at the kitchen you've inherited. By seeing beyond any obvious faults, you might discover some hidden potential and save yourself a hefty bill. If the counter and cabinet units are basically sound, for instance, but their color is dated or they look scratched, it's not difficult to repaint them and give them a facelift without the cost and inconvenience that comes with a major renovation. Scorched and scarred countertops are often the biggest problem in an old kitchen, so it's well worth investigating how much it will cost to replace them. For a country kitchen, real wood, or wood-look countertops appear warmer than glossy surfaces, although wood needs oiling regularly to keep it in peak condition. Replacing the cupboard doors is another option. Many companies will make new doors to fit your specifications, or, if you have basic carpentry skills, make your own plain doors using good-quality fiberboard.

The owners of this farmhouse kitchen have done very little to the original 1950's units that were there when they moved in 14 years ago. They painted the doors and shelving with shiny, hard-wearing gloss, and replaced the old countertops with low-cost pine, bleached with lye and sealed with Danish oil. Sprigged blue and white tiles over the countertop were put up at the same time, and the result is a retro-look country kitchen that has stood the test of time with far more character than a modern replacement.

LEFT: A farmhouse kitchen is a far cry from the clinical, minimalist look of many modern designs. Mugs hang from cup hooks, storage jars and jugs compete for space on the countertops, and visitors feel immediately at home when they sit at the fine old pine table.

Your kitchen units need to be thoroughly cleaned and sanded before you paint them. This task takes a little more time, but it's well worth it—you'll achieve a slick, long-lasting finish designed to withstand all the wear and tear of family life. After removing the handles, banish any residual dirt or grease by washing down the surfaces with a strong detergent and warm water. Sand lightly to prepare the surface for the paint, then use a suitable high-quality primer for the undercoat. When it dries, apply at least two coats of oil-based topcoat in a glossy or an eggshell finish. The paint will look smoother and more professional if you use a small foam roller rather than a brush, which can leave marks.

In this kitchen, the shelving and cupboard doors were painted white, and the drawer fronts and kickboard were coated with a soft shade of blue. The wall cupboards were given extra texture using masking tape to mark out a cross before hand-painting fine stripes in blue.

LEFT: The Swedish owner has used traditional Scandinavian decorating ideas to give her kitchen a feeling of the old country. Geraniums on the window ledge flower profusely all summer, and the curtains are kept deliberately short so they skim the tops of the plants.

RIGHT: The original kitchen range is now unused, but the black metal, kept polished and gleaming, makes a wonderful display area for pewter plates and china cups. Tiny calico hearts embroidered with cross-stitch kisses are another reminder of the home's Swedish heritage.

An open set of box shelves is set high on the wall and holds everything from egg cups to cans.

FLEA MARKET FINDS

Real shoestring-kitchen enthusiasts rarely buy anything new. They use what they already have and combine it with a mélange of cupboards, storage jars, and shelving that casts conventional ideas about taste and style to the four winds.

Your kitchen's style will evolve in an instant when you add in new treasures. Scour flea markets for hidden gems, and buy them on the spot. The best bargain-hunting relies on quick thinking and the thrill of a fast decision: if you ponder for days over whether or not to take that great cupboard you've found, it will probably be gone by the time you've made up your mind.

France is a fabulous hunting ground for flea market finds, and the owners of this unashamedly shoestring French kitchen have used everything from a discarded modern shelf unit (cut down, painted, and used as storage under the window) to a collection of cupboards and shelves stacked together on the walls. The color scheme of red, white, and blue keeps the room looking fresh, and the jumble of utensils, herbs, spices, bowls of fruit, and potted plants adds excitement, inspiring cooks to roll up their sleeves and get to work.

Below the shelves, hooks allow pans and colanders to drip dry into the traditional French ceramic sink.

The red-and-white striped café curtains are nonchalantly strung across the window on a wire.

Cut down to size and painted red and white, an inexpensive shelf unit makes another set of shelves under the window to hold baskets of home-grown vegetables.

Dried beans and rice in Mason jars; sugar cubes, lentils, and garlic cloves in pullout glass drawers—these staples, displayed in glass containers, are easy to spot when you're running low on supplies. The cooks in this kitchen like to see at a glance where everything is, and have filled up all available wall space and every countertop with the ingredients for their cooking, instead of hiding them away. Dried chili peppers have been threaded on twine for easy access, and a set of enamel storage jars in blue and white hold tea, coffee, and *tisanes*. The inside of the glass cupboard has been painted a vibrant blue with a piece of gingham pinned simply to the front.

RIGHT: *Simple flowers work best in a Shaker-style kitchen. An elegant square glass vase and a few dark pink tulips that echo the colors in the striped curtains are all that's needed.*

FAR RIGHT: *This small galley kitchen has been made to seem much bigger than it really is. Walls are lined with tongue-and-groove paneling and painted off-white, and peg rails, instead of wall cupboards, expand the sense of space even more.*

SHAKER STYLE

With its plain, unadorned design, Shaker style has become a classic for modern living, used for kitchens by everyone from the most illustrious design companies to the discount store on the corner. The ingredients of a Shaker kitchen are simplicity itself: plain doors without fancy moldings, turned wooden doorknobs, and peg rails for hanging utensils and cups. Wood painted in colors like cream, pale blue, or sometimes deep red are the most popular, topped by a real wooden countertop.

When it came to designing her kitchen, the owner of this small cottage was looking for Shaker style on a budget, but she wanted something more interesting than the plastic molded cupboard fronts which were all she could afford. The solution came when she had standard cupboard cabinets fitted, and ordered ready-made fiberboard doors that she could paint herself in pale blue.

A simple kitchen needs simple styling to keep its clean lines. Mason jars (top left) make a great alternative to wall cupboards for storing dry goods and, shown to the right, a set of simple shelves holds a collection of mid-twentieth-century Poole pottery that cries out to be admired. Below, rails for a slate message board and a pair of painted chairs at the small pine table complete the vintage look.

KITCHEN FINDS

In a French vacation home, a stone arch leads to a beamed kitchen where the owners have made no attempt to re-create the fitted kitchen they have in the city. Utilizing the most basic equipment, the kitchen relies upon a large wooden counter, open storage, and old aluminum kitchenware picked up on weekly shopping trips to the local market town, where the family take delight in searching for bargains. For only a few cents each, outdated colanders and patterned trivets are impossible to resist. Just a couple would be enough to use, but when hung from hooks on the wall, their intricate punched patterns and shapes are appreciated for their appearance.

You can turn the most boring utensils into a witty and unusual collection. Keep an eye out for vintage pieces and hang them together, so that small variations in design can play off each other. You'll be surprised at how many different shapes of cheese graters you can find, while wire whisks and even metal bottle openers can be far more interesting in juxtaposition than they ever looked in the kitchen drawer.

The antique open shelf over the sink was a junkyard find. It holds pan lids and glass tumblers that can be washed and put into place without drying.

A modern ceramic sink is suspended on a wooden frame, with no pretense of looking streamlined or sophisticated.

A wooden painted shop counter from England holds necessities like pots and pans, and its scrubbed top becomes a surface for chopping and mixing.

CHECKS AND STRIPES

Simple patterns like ginghams, checks, and stripes have always found their way into the kitchen. Traditionally woven in cotton, these unassuming patterns adorn fabrics that can be quickly washed and pressed, which is especially important, as they are often used to make tablecloths, napkins, and dishcloths. They are inexpensive, too—you can buy yards cheaply and then make them up into serviceable home textiles. The current vogue for Swedish style means that unlined valance, curtains, and simple roller blinds have replaced heavy drapes at windows throughout the house, however at a kitchen window they look especially fresh and pretty.

It's traditional in Europe and Scandinavia for a bare window to be framed by a checked or striped valance gathered onto a wire across the top, and the German owner of this kitchen has softened the contours of her tall window with a striped valance. You can achieve the same look in your own kitchen, but if you want to keep your privacy, add a plain white roller blind hung behind your valance.

OPPOSITE PAGE: *The tall kitchen window in this French house looks out over a big garden, so there's no need to put up curtains or blinds.*

BELOW: *The stripe of the curtain fabric shown opposite is echoed in the paint colors used on the wall. A simple device like painting a darker color below the dado height can change the proportions in a tall, narrow room.*

Not so long ago there were very few checked fabrics on the market, but these days you can buy an infinite variety of fabrics in hundreds of different colors. They are perfect for using throughout the house, from the living room and bedroom to the breakfast room and kitchen. If you have high windows, you'll maximize their elegance by letting your curtains fall right to the ground—cutting them off at the sill can look clumsy and truncated, and works better for smaller windows. When making floor-length curtains, don't allow them to be too full because less fabric means they'll hang neatly when they are drawn back. Tie-on seat covers can dress up country chairs and are practical at a dining table, as they can be easily removed and washed. If you are using Indian cottons for curtains or seat covers, be sure to wash the fabric before it's made up, as it will shrink.

LEFT: In the dining area of a country kitchen, floor-length cotton curtains coordinate with the practical painted cupboard and traditional glass lamp that hangs over the table.

RIGHT: A splash of color is added with serviceable seat covers made from dark blue-and-white cotton ticking. Originally used solely for mattress covers, ticking is now available in many different colors and always looks fresh and clean.

MAKING A SEAT COVER

Trace the top of the seat, including struts, onto tracing paper. Add 6 in. at the front and back for overhangs, plus ¾-in. turnings all around. Cut out one piece. Calculate the length of the side pieces by measuring from the center back to the front leg; make the depth 6 in. Add ¾ in. for turnings. With the right sides facing, join the ends of the side pieces to the sides of the front-edge overhang. Join the tops of the side pieces to the sides of the seat. Stitch a ¼-in. double hem around all the raw edges, clipping notches into the corners. Keep the seat cover in place with Velcro on the back edges of the side flaps, and add tape to tie the cover to the struts.

Checks may be used in
many guises all round the
house, and always add a
vibrant patch of color and
pattern. For instant charm
and style, try using dark
blue and white tiles to
make a checkerboard over
the sink—the simple
pattern is reflected in the
panes of the window and
in the checks on the
dishcloth. You can
transform a small wicker
table that has seen better
days by replacing the rotted
cane top with wood and
painting a checked game
board on it.

SUMMER RETREAT

Shoestring decorating means coming up with low-cost solutions that make a house easy to live in, and look beautiful, too. Where there's limited choice, sometimes all you can do is remove old floor coverings and sand the floorboards. This is especially practical in the kitchen, where a bare floor is easy to keep clean and makes any room look spacious. Bare boards can be painted with floor paint, bleached and oiled with Danish oil, or simply sealed with acrylic floor varnish. In this coastal summer retreat, the oiled floorboards make sure no one worries when the family traipses in from sailing with wet shoes.

LEFT: Colors in the kitchen reflect the blue of the open skies and the soft pink seen in rosy sunsets outside the windows of this vacation home, while the pale, sandy shades of the wooden furniture remind visitors of the wide beaches just over the dunes outside.

RIGHT: Keeping things simple was important to this family, so open shelves under the countertop have been hidden behind a pink striped curtain. This idea could be extended all around a kitchen if built-in cupboards are too expensive. Choose a cotton fabric that is easily washed, and hang curtains on wires.

Vintage buys add character to any room, and even a pair of faded, fifty-year-old curtains can grace a window with old-style charm. If they don't exactly fit, it's easy to shorten them, or you could add a plain hem to make them longer.

Enamel storage jars and bread boxes give a vintage look to any kitchen and are still relatively easy to find. Look for china cups and saucers, too—they can be planted with a hyacinth and garnished with a swirl of dried thyme secured with a hairpin.

Display utensils with panache, and you'll make your kitchen a welcoming place to cook and eat. Utensils hung on wall racks are ready to use, while wooden spoons clustered in a seaside bucket save rummaging in the drawer when you need them. The old-fashioned hutch is the epitome of a country kitchen and immediately says "home."

BLUES AND GREENS

Use blues and greens in your kitchen and you'll feel relaxed and cheerful every time you walk in. If initially you don't feel confident about using these colors, take a tip from nature and see how green foliage in a garden works with every color under the sun, while the bright blue of a summer sky always lifts your spirits and enhances everything it touches. And, as the bounty of the garden is brought straight to the kitchen table, it's only natural for kitchen colors to mirror the world outside. A vase of bright orange flowers on the table adds a splash of complementary color that gives even more of a zing to the room.

ABOVE: A set of new mugs and a few retro plates make a colorful combination at tea time. Mixing old and new means that you can pick up china for your kitchen whenever you spot a bargain.

FAR LEFT: : Color-washed blue walls and a sea-green hutch make bold statements in this kitchen, but the strong colors are tempered by plenty of white on the cabinets and table top.

LEFT: Slightly distressed and looking as if it's had plenty of use, a small glass-fronted cupboard contrasts with the blue walls and is very useful for storing tea and coffee.

BEDROOMS

Design yourself a romantic bedroom to be a haven of peace and tranquility at the end of a long day.

YOUNG AT HEART

When it comes to summer decorating, it's time to play with fabrics, yarns, and colors to make a bright and breezy bedroom that gives you space to dream. Replacing heavy drapes with light, airy sheers allows the sun to stream in throughout the day. You can find brightly colored muslins and lawns in dress fabric departments, or look for ready-made sheers and suspend them from bamboo poles in the most simple, unstructured way. Make the most of the transparent quality of the fabric by layering colors at the window, one on top of the other, for a gauzy, dreamy effect that looks terrific and costs very little.

LEFT AND BELOW CENTER: Nothing could be easier to install than this bamboo pole held up to the window by a pair of cup hooks. Two pairs of muslin curtains, in yellow and pink, are tied to the pole with fabric ties.

BELOW RIGHT: Play with color when you crochet: Start with easy squares and patch them together to make an Afghan cushion that uses up scraps of yarn.

TEXTILE TREASURES

Antique textile fairs are becoming more and more popular, selling everything from patchwork quilts to monogrammed linen sheets. Sometimes you can get lucky and unearth a beautiful old textile in a country antique shop, but as more dealers are snapping them up and exporting them from their country of origin, these days you are more likely to find the most beautiful pieces at specialty fairs. But take heart—it's still possible to find 1930's embroidered tray cloths or lace-trimmed pillowcases hidden amongst a pile of old clothes at a tag sale. For example, French markets always have the potential to surprise a serious textile hunter, and even the smallest piece of linen or embroidered cotton can be turned into a cushion cover or lavender sachet.

LEFT: Linen pillowcases, a pair of faded quilts, and a cotton crocheted cushion cover soften the lines of a metal daybed in the corner of this French bedroom.

BELOW: Yellowing buttons collected over the years, each one with a different design, decorate the corners of a linen lavender sachet; a pile of quilts waits to be put away after laundering.

If you are short on space at home but still want to enjoy having friends and family visit, why not be creative with what you have and turn a summer house or potting shed into a guest room for the summer? Whitewashed and filled with shoestring comforts, this stone building in an enclosed, walled garden was transformed in an afternoon when the owners needed another bedroom in a hurry. The elements are simple: a shelf unit made from wooden planking, a peg rail to hang clothes, and a big bed that completely fills the space.

A garden bedroom can be a delight on hot nights, and guests will be able to enjoy the sounds and scents of the garden as they drift off to sleep. Make sure there's a flask for early morning tea or coffee, and treat them to a pile of fluffy towels and plenty of books.

OPPOSITE: With freshly laundered sheets, and plenty of warm blankets and quilts in case the night turns chilly, what could be more inviting than a bedroom in the garden?

BELOW LEFT: The simplest set of shelves is placed against the wall and holds a few home comforts: a tin of cookies, a flask for hot drinks, and a vase of freshly cut roses from the garden.

BELOW RIGHT: There's no room for a closet or wardrobe, so a chunky peg rail over the end of the bed gives guests somewhere to hang clothes.

A shelf hung high above the bed holds a table lamp that many people would have simply thrown away (the original shade was tattered beyond repair). The wrought-iron base, however, works perfectly, making the piece ideal for a shoestring "rescue and refurb." After snipping away the old fabric, the frame was decorated with silk flowers threaded through the base, which soften the light of the bare bulb. The lamp is placed high enough over the bed for the light not to be glaring, and the wrought-iron mirror behind it allows more light to be reflected back into the room.

VINTAGE BEDROOMS

The secret of vintage-style bedrooms is their simple, natural feel. Where wall-to-wall carpets and heavy drapes would overwhelm, plaster walls, scrubbed wooden floors, and unstructured window dressings provide the perfect setting for restored secondhand furniture. Old metal beds are now fetching astronomical prices in cities. Yet in the countryside, their counterparts can sometimes be acquired for very little. All the beds in this house were bought for a song, but their true beauty started to emerge only after they were cleaned of rust and painted in pale colors.

FAR LEFT: *A folding metal campaign bed, used in the nineteenth century for the military, has been covered in a faded striped coverlet and makes a wonderful daybed with a pair of fluffy pillows.*

BOTTOM LEFT: *Wildflowers look fresh and natural when placed in an old enamel jug, proving that the best things in life are free.*

In an attic bedroom with a sharply-sloping ceiling, it can be difficult to find storage items to fit the space—but let your imagination roam, and you'll come up with some ingenious solutions. These homemade coat hangers will hold light clothing, and are whimsically strung between two beams to fill an irregular space. To make them, whittle curved ends from sticks and wrap wire around the stick tightly, bending the free end into a hook.

Another problem in a roofspace is arranging furniture within the constraints of the sloping ceiling. But beds don't have to be pushed against a wall: To appreciate the charm of a delicate, cast-iron frame, pull a high double bed out into the room and use a country chair as a bedside table. An old quilt may be almost in tatters, but it looks wonderful displayed across the bed, and the end of the bed is the perfect place to throw a cotton robe. Close under the eaves, a low chest painted in glossy robin's egg blue provides ample storage as well as a place to display treasured objects like a pretty lamp, a homemade wooden boat, and a modest little mirror.

Pinned in place across a window, a linen monogrammed sheet is tied back during the day. The mosquito net over the bed at night is strictly practical; draped back in the morning, it looks so romantic.

A seashell tie-back is child's play to put together. Adding creative and beautiful details like these gives a summer bedroom charm and character.

A hayrack found in the farm buildings by the house makes a statement as a hanging rack for towels and shirts.

In a pale-colored room, the blue wrought-iron bed's delightful curves contrast with the simple navy-and-white gingham quilt folded at the foot.

Doubling as a bedside table for books and cups of coffee, the wooden chest also provides useful storage for blankets and quilts.

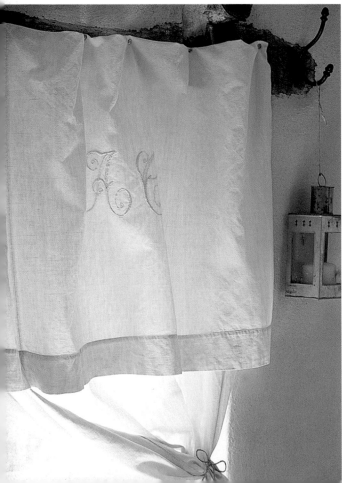

MIXING PATTERNS

Fabrics printed with pastoral scenes are as popular today as they were in the eighteenth century, when they were first produced. Although first developed in Ireland in 1752, the French soon learned the printing technique, and the best of these fabrics came from the famous Oberkampf mill in Jouy. Classical designs and pastoral scenes were popular, and both Benjamin Franklin and George Washington imported toiles for use in their homes. In fact, the original furnishings for the White House in Washington D.C. included toiles de Jouy. Today, toiles have become a design classic, and rooms decorated with these all-over patterns can look grand and luxurious. Toiles printed with pastoral scenes will mix happily with unassuming checks and stripes, and look especially pretty in bedrooms.

The wallpaper and curtains of this French rectory were already in place when the owners moved in, and it was only by chance that they survived a week-long flood that destroyed most of the wallpaper in the rest of the house. With the other bedrooms now painted in plain colors, the riot of pattern in the master bedroom has been toned down with simple, country fabrics that add charm and novelty.

OPPOSITE: *A small bedroom chair, covered in blue and white stripes, sits in front of the window with its sumptuous views of the French countryside.*

ABOVE LEFT: *A scalloped pelmet is trimmed with pompom braid that makes a charming heading for the floor-length curtains.*

LEFT: *Red gingham cotton fabric, used to cover the shaped headboard, looks crisp and fresh against the toile wallpaper.*

OPPOSITE: *A curve sliced out of the corners of this wooden headboard means the ornate carved panel found a home at last.*

BELOW: *Painted freehand in cool sea greens and blues, wobbly stripes and spots make an inexpensive white lampshade look special.*

A little lateral thinking can make the most of quite ordinary objects. Decorated by hand or given a new decorative finish, it's amazing how a personalized lampshade or headboard can give a bedroom instant character. Shoestring decorators will never pass by a seemingly unusable junk-shop find, but will fall in love with its beauty and take it home to wait for a suitable place to display it. Neither will they pass by a bargain if the sales yield a particularly tempting offer. This carved panel (shown on right), originally taken from the back of a chiffoniere or sideboard, was an exciting find, but gathered dust in the corner of the attic until it found rightful employment as a carved pediment for a characterless wooden headboard. A home-store-bought table lamp, on the other hand, was purchased purely as an inexpensive and cheerful accessory to light a dark corner. Its white base and plain paper shade lacked appeal, so they were hand-painted with fun stripes and spots using artist's acrylic colors.

SCANDINAVIAN STYLE

In Scandinavian countries like Norway, Denmark, and Sweden, the winters are long and dark, so traditionally, country interiors have been designed to let in as much light as possible. Light, whitewashed rooms create a sense of space, and simple furniture painted in pale colors with bleached wooden floors that reflect the light are typical ingredients of this style. The look is fresh and tranquil, and is easy to re-create on a shoestring.

At the windows, try hanging unlined muslins from the simplest wooden curtain pole to let in light unimpeded. Where possible, let curtains drift to the floor so they can billow at the open window during warm summer breezes. Furniture needs to be plain and unfussy—paint it white or gray, or bleach it for an aged effect before positioning it sparingly around the room. For beautifully pale floors, bleach out the yellow from bare floorboards, and oil the wood. A couple of woven cotton runners keep the look pure and simple.

LEFT: All the furniture in this farmhouse bedroom has been given a bleached look, while simple stripes of blue add a crisp finish.

RIGHT: Ribbon-trimmed white muslin curtains and a pair of generous-size pillows positioned under the window add a sense of symmetry to the room.

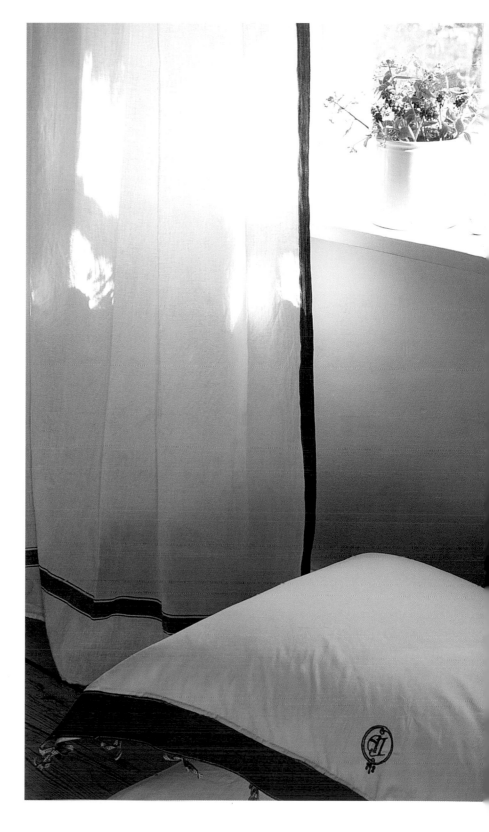

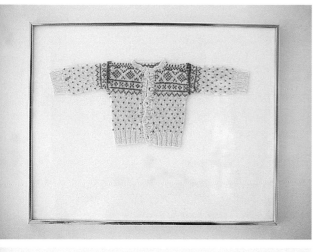

A collection of carefully chosen pots on a mantel and a baby's cardigan in a frame add texture and nostalgia. For a real Scandinavian look, you can add mock paneling to white walls by painting on lines of color. Mark a rectangle on the wall using masking tape, and position another line of tape within it. Paint between the tapes and peel off when dry. Continue by painting another rectangle inside the first in the same way.

ARTS AND CRAFTS

In the early part of the twentieth century, artists Vanessa Bell and Duncan Grant, part of the Bloomsbury group of artists and writers, moved to Charleston in Sussex, England, where they spent the following half-century decorating their house in their own inimitable way. Walls, fireplaces, furniture, and ceramics were all decorated in a free and colorful style.

By painting the walls of your bedroom in a glorious patchwork of color and pattern, you'll create art that is miles ahead of conventional wallpaper—and make a room that is as individual as you are. A white wall makes a wonderful bare canvas, so experiment with patches of color, overlaying them with painted textures in coordinating shades of stripes, chevrons, circles, and diamonds. It's so easy to paint out any section you're not happy with and start again. If you're not used to working with colors, make a scrapbook of postcards, magazine cuttings, and photographs that inspire you, or choose a small palette of sample colors from the same paint range and experiment on paper before you begin.

FAR LEFT: *This bedroom in an authentic Arts and Crafts house has been hand-painted by decorator Annabel Grey. The original fireplace with its copper hood, and the dressing table found in a secondhand store, give the room a look of the period, but the innovative wall treatment is in a class of its own.*

LEFT: *Painted in a selection of subtle yellows, blues, and grays, with white and silver leaf, the walls shimmer as the light moves around the room.*

LEFT: *Put in a simple frame, a pretty scrap of embroidery looks wonderful leaning on the mantelpiece, but it's the juxtaposition of objects that gives the display its panache: a single piece of driftwood, a pair of vintage shoes, and the bottom half of an old oil lamp make an eclectic collection.*

ABOVE RIGHT: *Lloyd loom chairs have been made ever since 1907, when an American named Marshall Burns Lloyd invented a loom that could weave twisted craft paper into a woven fabric reinforced with steel wire. Lloyd loom furniture has been popular ever since, and it's easy to find slightly battered chairs that can be sprayed or kept as they are.*

BOTTOM RIGHT: *You can spot an original Arts and Crafts piece by the hearts and other shapes cut out of the woodwork. Expect to pay a high price for a real antique, but a more modest dressing table from the 1930s or '40s would make a fine place to display an array of small vases in the corner of the bedroom.*

Confident decorating doesn't always mean finding a style and sticking to it. It can be so much more fun to decorate a room with nothing to go on but your personal whims. Just follow your instincts and look for colors and objects that speak to you. Breaking free of the tyranny of interior style can be liberating, and you will eventually find your own personal style by constantly searching and refining—after all, if you are a true shoestring shopper, nothing you buy will have cost a fortune, and it can all be passed on or given to a secondhand store if you decide to get rid of it later

If you can't live without the bronze Buddha's hand you brought back from Thailand, or that tinkling set of wind chimes made in Bali, why not use them as accessories in your bedroom, even if they seem to be worlds apart from the style you thought you wanted. Eclectic collecting is the name of the game, and the best finds can be discovered wherever you go. Browsing through a Sunday flea market in your home town might find you leaving with a vintage eiderdown that just needs a trip to the dry cleaners to make it worthy of a place on your bed. A visit to a foreign bazaar is bound to have you return home with more than you took with you, and even your local garage sale might yield an unwanted drinking glass that would look lovely sitting on your dressing table, filled with a bouquet of spring flowers.

BATHROOMS

When you carry out shoestring ideas, your bathroom gets creative accessories and a fresh, country feel.

WASHED IN BY THE SEA

A stroll along the beach can be paradise for shoestring decorators. Here you can find driftwood to decorate your home. In the bathroom, especially, driftwood comes into its own. Look along the high-tide mark for pale-toned wood cast out by the sea, and you'll discover a source of wonderful inspiration.

If you live near the beach and are an old hand at beachcombing, take home some planks of driftwood. Fitted together to make shelves, or used to hide ugly water pipes behind a narrow cupboard, they will give an outdoor feel even to a newly built apartment. If visiting the beach is limited to your annual vacation, bring home some scraps of driftwood and glue them around the edges of an old mirror frame, or use them, au naturel, as an unstructured soap dish on the washstand.

For a beach-like feel in the bathroom, choose pale painted wood. You can use tongue-and-groove paneling washed with a thin coat of white water-based paint and sealed with acrylic varnish for a bleached, natural look. Giving wood a couple of protective coats of white glossy paint will result in a more contemporary effect, but as with painted wooden floorboards, years of family life will undoubtedly result in a scuffed, well-worn look that no clever paint effect can re-create. Be inspired by the colors of the sea, too, and hand-paint the sides of the bathtub in washes of brilliant blues and greens that emulate the far-distant horizon.

ABOVE: A humorous shelf bracket has been made from a piece of wood cut into the shape of a fish. On the shelf, a pair of model lighthouses, toy boats, and a collection of blue and white tiles make a lighthearted seaside display.

RIGHT: White walls and white-painted wood, contrasting with the vivid colors of the bath and cotton rug, give this small bathroom an amazing impact that instantly recalls walks by the ocean in summer.

MOSAIC MAGIC

From the time of the ancient Greeks in the fourth century B.C., mosaics have been used for decorating surfaces like floors, walls, and ceilings. The techniques are easy enough for anyone to succeed with, allowing you to make vibrant surfaces of broken color that give an individual touch to any room. As materials you can buy ready-made mosaic glass tiles, use small pieces of broken china and mirrored glass, or even use a collection of buttons. For a simple mosaic surface, break china or mirrored glass inside a cloth bag to avoid flying pieces, or snip them with tile cutters into the shapes you want, and always wear goggles to protect your eyes. Arrange the pieces, and when you are happy with the result, attach the pieces to a nonporous surface using PVA glue. Grout between the gaps in the pieces, and allow it to dry.

RIGHT: A fabulous mosaic bath panel, made by decorator Annabel Grey, turns a tiny bathroom into an Aladdin's cave of pattern and color.

BELOW LEFT: This button mirror is a wonderful flight of fancy with its round shape and radiating button decoration.

BELOW RIGHT: Here, Annabel used a combination of shapes cut from mirror glass, china, and wall tiles in a variety of clear colors.

Flat pebbles from the beach make a natural border for a large piece of mirrored glass.

A dented aluminum flask from a thrift shop is used as a whimsical vase on the tiled shelf.

Roughly formed wooden doors have been coated with a thin wash of color that blends in naturally with the pebble-mosaic cupboard.

A wooden cupboard, decorated like the mirror frame with flat pebbles, continues the beach theme.

RIGHT: *You can buy glass tesserae and ceramic tiles from mosaic suppliers to decorate large projects as well as smaller objects, like this bottle and clock. Simple designs work best on smaller objects, but pieces may need to be staggered to fit around curved edges.*

Use your shoestring decorating skills to seek out accessories, and make your bathroom unique and welcoming. A piece of faded toile fabric softens a Lloyd loom chair, a battered enamel bowl makes a simple soap dish, and a recycled jug, used for carrying water in the era before indoor plumbing, is beautiful as a simple vase.

A bathroom mirror is a necessity, but there is no reason why it can't make an attractive contribution to the decorating scheme as well. This ornate- framed mirror gives the

bathroom a feminine look. An
antique boot stretcher makes a
witty holder for toilet paper rolls. A
simple vase of fragrant flowers adds
instant color to any bathroom.

LETTING IN THE LIGHT

Make creative choices, and your bathroom will be more than a "useful but boring" room. As with all shoestring decorating, using objects in unusual ways is what transforms them from the ordinary into the magical. One mirror is useful and necessary, but cover the wall in mirrors, and something special happens to the light as it's reflected from a variety of shapes and sizes. Think differently when it comes to window dressing, too. A square of muslin is all that's needed to filter the light coming through a bathroom window—but pin up an antique linen dishcloth, and the window becomes a focal point. It's just a matter of creative thinking and a lighthearted touch.

ABOVE: The hand-woven stripe and tiny monogram on this linen dishcloth are hung up at eye level to be admired.

RIGHT: You don't need to look for special antiques to make a unique collection of mirrors; choose a medley of beveled mirrors, ordinary wooden frames, and a modern chrome mirror.

MAKING A SANCTUARY

A bathroom can be so much more than just a place to wash. At the end of a hard day, the thought of a blissful haven will make you look forward to coming home. By focusing on the senses, you can transform even a plain country bathroom into a sanctuary. For a sensual ambience, keep the lighting low by placing candles around the tub. A blend of essential oils like bergamot, lavender, chamomile, and clary sage added to warm bath water release a wonderful fragrance that will relax you as you soak. Play soothing classical music to help unwind, and keep a pile of soft, fluffy towels on hand to wrap around you as you step out of the bath.

FAR RIGHT: *None of the ingredients in this simple bathroom is expensive. The tea lights in glass votive holders give a pleasing and relaxing ambience that makes the room feel like a health spa. The piece of coral lit up by the candle suggests a grotto and casts interesting shadows on the wall above.*

RIGHT: *Keep a soft towel and sweet-smelling soaps on a chair pulled up close to the bath so you can reach them easily.*

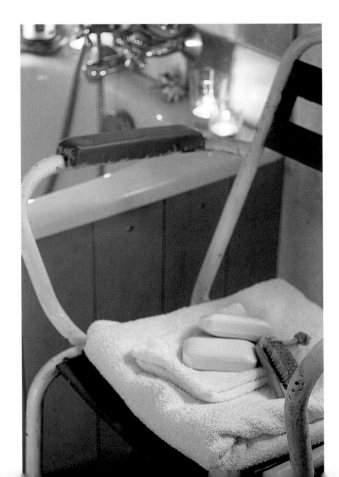

LEFT: *In this tiny bathroom, a wooden hanging rack is lowered from the ceiling on a system of pulleys that makes it easy for wet towels to be hung up to dry .*

FACING PAGE: *The simplest storage solutions are often the best. Here, a set of wire vegetable baskets, designed for use in a kitchen, have been hung in a bathroom window and used to store toiletries.*

CREATIVE STORAGE

Whether you have a tiny bathroom that allows room only for the bare essentials, or a large family bathroom with enough floor area to accommodate an easy chair, good storage is always important. Organized storage means a tidier bathroom; it's easier to wash there, and in turn, your life feels simpler and calmer. With a few key storage solutions in place, you can begin to introduce soothing extras like candles, flowers, and scented oils (see page 130); in contrast a bathroom filled with jars, bottles, and wet towels will just make you dash in for a quick shower and out again, rushing at a time that could otherwise have been spent enjoying valuable personal space.

It's always tempting to want to store things below when they need a home, but looking upwards can be the first step in solving any storage problems. Wall spaces can be used for shelving. Hooks, racks, and even hanging baskets will help you to organize bathroom necessities, making it easy to find things when you need them. Why not look for creative solutions to storing the array of shampoos, bottles, hairsprays, toothpaste, and face creams that always seem to be waiting to cover every available surface? See-through hanging baskets made from wire or plastic can be filled with necessities, and will appear to take up less space than more solid materials. Places to store clean towels and dirty laundry are a must, or your bathroom floor will become a dumping ground. The easiest solution can be a simple coat hook on the back of the door, so be on the lookout for old hooks in junk shops. Even bent and rusty ones can be cleaned up and will add character to a room. Any bathroom will benefit from a Shaker-style peg rail on the wall for storing a set of color-coded laundry bags, one for each member of the family, while an old-fashioned creel, or hanging rack, is perfect for keeping wet towels off the floor while they dry.

If you have the luxury of a spacious bathroom, it can be tempting to bring in lots of small storage units and place them around the room—and inadvertently create a new kind of clutter. By choosing floor-to-ceiling built-in cupboards, you'll benefit from plenty of hanging space for clothes, shelving for towels, drawers for toiletries, and room for a large laundry basket that can be tucked neatly away behind closed doors. For a shoestring alternative, buy a cheap flat-pack storage system and assemble it along one wall, or look for similar junk-shop furniture—paint the pieces the same color, add matching handles, and stack one on top of another. Sand and prime old wooden cupboards first, and make sure that they are grease-free before painting.

LEFT: *Here, slate floor tiles make a practical and beautiful backsplash for a traditional-looking basin and taps in this spacious bathroom. The countertop was a salvaged piece of slate taken from an old pantry.*

RIGHT: *A spare bedroom has been turned into a bathroom in this 1930's house. The fitted cupboards, modeled on the original paneled doors throughout the house, have been painted to match the walls in a strong off-white.*

A creative way to utilize your bathroom storage is to make a habit of displaying collections of just about anything. A set of ceramic pots or a set of colored glass jars, arranged on the window ledge, can hold everything from cotton balls to hairpins, and will add valuable storage space to the tiniest corner. A set of small enamel buckets, a quirky collection of vintage tins, or even a few lidded baskets all serve a dual purpose of hiding away knickknacks, as well as providing a point of interest. Useful products like bath scrubs, foot gels, and exfoliating pumice stones can be mixed with natural objects on a shelf to make an eye-catching arrangement.

BELOW LEFT: A pair of seagrass boxes add interesting texture, but also provide useful storage.

BELOW RIGHT: Installed above the bath where they can easily be reached, these shelves hold sponges, soaps, and lotions. An interesting mix of objects, from seashells to dried leaves, enlivens the otherwise utilitarian space.

BELOW LEFT: To make attractive clothes hangers, cut fabric one-and-a-half times the length of a wooden hanger and use running stitches to gather it to fit.

BELOW RIGHT: Matching ties close the top of this drawstring laundry bag. Its white trim becomes a simple frill when the drawstrings are gathered.

If you enjoy sewing, think of creative ways to use natural fabrics to make useful storage items for the bathroom that also look pretty. A set of padded coat hangers covered with linen will help store crisply pressed white shirts and keep shoulders in shape, and look far more attractive than plain wooden or plastic hangers. A decorative laundry bag, made from blue and white toile de Jouy, or whatever other scraps of fabric you have on hand, will hide away socks while they wait for the wash, and add a splash of color to your bathroom.

RAG-BAG CHIC

LEFT: *If you don't have enough fabric to make a cushion, use three strips of scrap joined together. Vintage buttons taken from recycled shirts give the cushion added texture.*

BELOW: *Trim a fluffy towel with a narrow strip of pattern. It's a great way to personalize towels for different family members.*

When you sew for the bathroom, you don't need to waste a scrap of fabric. You can use even the slimmest pickings from your rag bag to patch together a cushion cover or decorate a hand towel. The bathroom usually has little space for patterned fabrics, but introducing small areas of pattern will give the décor a homespun feel. Patterns that coordinate with your color scheme will also add detail, and beautifully unite disparate elements of the room.

OUTDOORS

With a creative eye and some clever shoestring shopping, you can turn your backyard into an inspired outdoor room.

GARDEN LIVING

Whether you have a large backyard or just a tiny balcony in the city, it's well worth making yourself a peaceful haven to relax in after the hustle and bustle of the day. Maximizing your outdoor space means enjoying all its potential—from the first cup of coffee of the day to a moment of stargazing on a balmy night.

Battered old folding director's chairs are easy to find and, with a new canvas cover and a coat of paint, make a comfortable place to sit. Make full use of potted plants that can be moved into the sun as they come into flower and tucked away in the winter while they regenerate for next year.

OPPOSITE: A quiet corner of a garden catches the early evening sun—just the place for sipping a glass of wine.

BELOW LEFT: The original canvas on this director's chair has been replaced, but two or three hot summers have faded the colors to mellow tones.

BELOW RIGHT: The smallest outdoor space can be a riot of color. This window onto the street is bursting with pots that spill over onto the seat below.

When it gets dark, there's no need to abandon your outdoor living area. Use candles and fairy lights to illumine a table and create a twinkling grotto to welcome guests. A night-light in a jelly jar strung with string makes the simplest lantern and keeps the delicate flame protected from the breeze. Small fabric bags, tops folded back and filled with sand, glow with color when they are lit up; paper bags with a base of sand and a tiny candle inside become wonderful pillars of light, but make sure these are only used outside. On still evenings, you can place a candle in a scallop shell and give each place setting an individual pool of light.

GREEN THUMBS

There's nothing like your own garden for experiencing the simple pleasures of life, and what could be more satisfying than picking home-grown herbs, or twisting a wreath from dried flowers you have grown yourself? Gardening can mean caring for wide-open spaces with green lawns and trees, or it can be a rich tapestry of planting that invites us to bend down and examine it close up. Get to know plants that originate from alpine meadows, and plant them together to form a magic carpet of texture and color. Alpines love well-drained soil, so mix in plenty of grit when planting and spread gravel around each plant to prevent the leaves from rotting. The aroma of herbs like rosemary, thyme, lemon balm, and bay are at their most pungent in the hot sun, but if possible, keep a tub of herbs near the kitchen door so you can easily pick the leaves when you're cooking.

LEFT: *Gardening at its most simple: an enamel jar hanging from a shutter is planted with cosmos.*

RIGHT, CLOCKWISE: *A cracked and scarred ceramic sink found at the local recycling center is planted with jewel-like alpines that lift their faces to the sun. Hydrangea blooms, picked at their peak and left to dry in the sun, make a pretty wreath that will last until next summer. A 1930s enamel baby bath, found in a junk shop, nurtures a mass of fragrant herbs that are used for flavoring everything from soups to salads in the kitchen.*

DINING AT DUSK

After a hot day in the garden, it can be refreshing to serve dinner for friends in a shady conservatory, where fragrant plants give off a heady aroma in the evening. Look for strongly scented varieties of heliotrope like "Chatsworth" and "The Queen," with flowers that range from pale violet to purple and smell intoxicating. The jasmine family provides deliciously scented white flowers that hang like stars through shiny green leaves. Plant the Arabian jasmine "Sambac," which flowers almost continuously, or the highly scented "Angulaire," that can be persuaded to flower all year if it's given warm enough conditions. For brilliant color, bougainvillea can't be beat, so look for the dense pink flowers of "Chiang Mai Beauty," or the brighter magenta and white variety "Blushing Beauty."

Furniture for the conservatory can be simply eclectic; you'll find it at all the usual shoestring haunts, so there's no need for matching sets of pristine wicker or fancy painted metal tables. Snap up a bargain set of folding chairs at the local thrift store—if they are rusty and a bit squeaky, a little oil on their joints is all they need to become well-loved, useful additions to the garden or conservatory. A huge pine table that has seen better days can be restored with a touch of lye and Danish oil to feed the wood, and it creates a wonderfully bleached effect that goes nicely under flowering plants. Set the table with inexpensive china from the home section of any department store; a pure white dinner service is all you'll need. Pile up plates and cutlery with folded napkins and let dinner guests help themselves to dishes of fresh salads and glasses of chilled white wine, and put out plenty of candles to add a sparkle to the darkness as the light begins to fade.

ABOVE LEFT: *Don't be brokenhearted if you break a favorite candlestick. Glue the pieces together with a strong adhesive and bind it with ribbon threaded with a wooden heart.*

BOTTOM LEFT: *Candles are the key to any evening party, but using a glass storm lantern on the table can be costly. Make a shoestring version with a budget-priced glass vase and sit a large church candle in the bottom. Let the wax drip and pool in the base to add atmosphere and authenticity.*

RIGHT: *A conservatory is often the best place to have an outdoor dinner party, because it keeps out cool breezes and you won't have to cancel if a summer storm looms.*

Retro-style cotton fabrics printed with a riot of flowers turn a small backyard into a celebratory space for a tea party. If you're a competent sewer, you can create a pair of garden chair covers or a peg bag; beginners can tackle a set of flowery napkins, or cut out triangles with pinking shears to make a bright banner.

You can use a multitude of shoestring finds to turn your garden into an outdoor paradise. A wooden vegetable box, painted bright pink, makes useful extra seating, while a set of flat-pack shoe racks, painted in blue, transforms into a stylish plant rack. Almost anything will do as a plant container as long as you make a hole in the bottom before planting. Add a layer of gravel and good-quality compost, and feed regularly for a healthy display of flowers.

INDEX

ACKNOWLEDGMENTS

For my family

I would like to thank the following for letting us into their inspiring homes with such generosity and good humour:

Eva and Edward Johnson, Karen Nichol and Peter Clarke, Lizzie Hutton, Julia and Chris Cowper, Simon Finch, Cailey and Marlene Hutton, Susan Waller and Frederic Maurau, Charlie Pollard and Nicola Contreras, Roger and Belinda Bamber.

I would also like to say a big thank you to all those shops and suppliers who lent us props and gave so liberally of flowers and fabrics for the shoots:

Ark +44 1223 307676, Baileys Home and Garden +44 1989 563015,
Bed of Roses +44 1992 500390, Breeze +44 1223 354403,
Cabbages and Roses +44 1225 859151, Cath Kidston +44 207 893 7700,
Eleanor Yeats, Elizabeth David Cookshop +44 800 373792, Evolution +44 1223 868600,
The Hive 01223 300269, John Lewis +44 207 495 3541,
Malabar 0207 501 4200, Molton Brown +44 20 751 8430, Rowan +44 1484 681881,
Sasha Waddell +44 207 736 0766, Sandra Jane +44 1223 323211

Angel kits using the Kaffe Fassett fabric collection are available from Eleanor Yeats, tel +44 191 2529794
Trip Trap Danish Lye and oil available from Eva John, tel +44 1638 731362
Annabel Grey, decorator, tel +44 7860 500356
Ceramics by Nicola Contreras, tel +44 1206 385997